THE

PERIODIC TABLE...

Is Weird!

CONTENTS

LITTLE TIGER
LONDON

CATERPILLAR BOOKS
An imprint of the Little Tiger Group • www.littletiger.co.uk
1 Coda Studios, 189 Munster Road, London SW6 6AW
Imported into the EEA by Penguin Random House Ireland,
Morrison Chambers, 32 Nassau Street, Dublin DO2 YH68
First published in Great Britain 2022
Copyright © Noodle Fuel Ltd 2022
Text by Noodle Fuel Ltd 2022
Illustrations by Luke Newell 2022
All rights reserved • Printed in China
A CIP catalogue record of this book is available
from the British Library
ISBN: 978-1-83891-458-5 • CPB/2800/2113/0122
1 3 5 7 9 10 8 6 4 2

FSC
www.fsc.org
MIX
Paper from
responsible sources
FSC® C017606

The Forest Stewardship Council® (FSC®) is an
international, non-governmental organisation
dedicated to promoting responsible
management of the world's forests. FSC
operates a system of forest certification and
product labelling that allows consumers to
identify wood and wood-based products
from well-managed forests.

For more information about the FSC,
please visit their website at www.fsc.org.

Welcome to the weird and wonderful world of the periodic table of elements. Here at the Floortlesnazz Grobblesnot Intergalactic Scientific Institute, we have recently discovered a bizarre race of alien beings known as... HUMANS!

They're really quite interesting and we thought you might want to see what they've learnt so far about chemistry.

Humans are obviously not as advanced as us, but they have come up with a rather clever way of listing all the elements.

They call it the periodic table and you won't believe some of the weird things they've done with it!

THE PERIODIC TABLE

Elements are the building blocks that make **everything else** in the universe.

The periodic table is a way of **grouping together** all the elements in nature.

The elements are arranged by their **atomic number**, starting with hydrogen (1) and ending, for now at least, with oganesson (118).

NOW THAT IS A PROPER SCIENCE BEARD!

The first periodic table was created by Dmitri Mendeleev in **1869** to show how elements are organised.

1 **H** Hydrogen								
3 **Li** Lithium	4 **Be** Beryllium							
11 **Na** Sodium	12 **Mg** Magnesium							
19 **K** Potassium	20 **Ca** Calcium	21 **Sc** Scandium	22 **Ti** Titanium	23 **V** Vanadium	24 **Cr** Chromium	25 **Mn** Manganese	26 **Fe** Iron	27 **Co** Cobalt
37 **Rb** Rubidium	38 **Sr** Strontium	39 **Y** Yttrium	40 **Zr** Zirconium	41 **Nb** Niobium	42 **Mo** Molybdenum	43 **Tc** Technetium	44 **Ru** Ruthenium	45 **Rh** Rhodium
55 **Cs** Caesium	56 **Ba** Barium	57–71 Lanthanoids	72 **Hf** Hafnium	73 **Ta** Tantalum	74 **W** Tungsten	75 **Re** Rhenium	76 **Os** Osmium	77 **Ir** Iridium
87 **Fr** Francium	88 **Ra** Radium	89–103 Actinoids	104 **Rf** Rutherfordium	105 **Db** Dubnium	106 **Sg** Seaborgium	107 **Bh** Bohrium	108 **Hs** Hassium	109 **Mt** Meitnerium

An element's atomic number is the number of protons (a positively charged particle) that are found in the element's **nucleus**. A nucleus is the small, dense region of protons and neutrons at the centre of an atom.

57 **La** Lanthanum	58 **Ce** Cerium	59 **Pr** Praseodymium	60 **Nd** Neodymium	61 **Pm** Promethium	62 **Sm** Samarium
89 **Ac** Actinium	90 **Th** Thorium	91 **Pa** Protactinium	92 **U** Uranium	93 **Np** Neptunium	94 **Pu** Plutonium

electron

HYDROGEN

nucleus

neutron

proton

NITROGEN

KEY

Alkali Metal	Alkaline-earth Metal	Transition Metal	Base Metal	Metalloid

Each element in a group has the **same number** of electrons in its outer shell. This is what gives each element its group number. Having the same number of electrons also means each element in the group has similar properties and chemical reactions.

Elements that are not in specific groups, the **transition metals** for example, do not necessarily have the same number of electrons in their outer shell.

The **seven rows** of the table are known as periods and generally have metals on the left and non-metals on the right.

The columns are called groups and contain elements with **similar chemical behaviours**. For example, elements in group 17 are called the halogens and elements in group 18 are called the noble gases.

									2 **He** Helium
			5 **B** Boron	6 **C** Carbon	7 **N** Nitrogen	8 **O** Oxygen	9 **F** Fluorine	10 **Ne** Neon
			13 **Al** Aluminium	14 **Si** Silicon	15 **P** Phosphorus	16 **S** Sulfur	17 **Cl** Chlorine	18 **Ar** Argon
28 **Ni** Nickel	29 **Cu** Copper	30 **Zn** Zinc	31 **Ga** Gallium	32 **Ge** Germanium	33 **As** Arsenic	34 **Se** Selenium	35 **Br** Bromine	36 **Kr** Krypton
46 **Pd** Palladium	47 **Ag** Silver	48 **Cd** Cadmium	49 **In** Indium	50 **Sn** Tin	51 **Sb** Antimony	52 **Te** Tellurium	53 **I** Iodine	54 **Xe** Xenon
78 **Pt** Platinum	79 **Au** Gold	80 **Hg** Mercury	81 **Tl** Thallium	82 **Pb** Lead	83 **Bi** Bismuth	84 **Po** Polonium	85 **At** Astatine	86 **Rn** Radon
110 **Ds** Darmstadtium	111 **Rg** Roentgenium	112 **Cn** Copernicium	113 **Nh** Nihonium	114 **Fl** Flerovium	115 **Mc** Moscovium	116 **Lv** Livermorium	117 **Ts** Tennessine	118 **Og** Oganesson

63 **Eu** Europium	64 **Gd** Gadolinium	65 **Tb** Terbium	66 **Dy** Dysprosium	67 **Ho** Holmium	68 **Er** Erbium	69 **Tm** Thulium	70 **Yb** Ytterbium	71 **Lu** Lutetium
95 **Am** Americium	96 **Cm** Curium	97 **Bk** Berkelium	98 **Cf** Californium	99 **Es** Einsteinium	100 **Fm** Fermium	101 **Md** Mendelevium	102 **No** Nobelium	103 **Lr** Lawrencium

Non-metal	Halogens	Noble Gas	Rare Earth	Radioactive Rare Earth

SO, YOU'RE SAYING THAT NOBLE GASES AREN'T WHAT A KING FARTS?

PHUT

ATOMS, COMPOUNDS AND STATES OF MATTER

ATOMS

An atom is the **smallest** form of an element.

Each atom has a central core called a **nucleus** (made up of protons and neutrons). Electrons whizz in rings around the nucleus.

neutron

electron

Atoms are incredibly small, measuring only 0.0000001mm (0.000000001in), and can only be seen using **special microscopes**.

The number of **protons** gives the element its atomic number.

proton

nucleus

MICROSCOPE? WHAT'S A MICROSCOPE?

The total number of electrons **matches** the total number of protons in the nucleus.

IT'S OKAY, THERE'S NO CHARGE...

An atom is made up of **tiny particles** called protons, electrons and neutrons. The protons have a positive electric charge, the electrons have a negative electric charge and the neutrons have no electric charge.

PROTONS   ELECTRONS   NEUTRONS

COMPOUNDS

Most of the substances in the world are made up of **compounds**. Compounds are formed when atoms of different elements join together to form molecules.

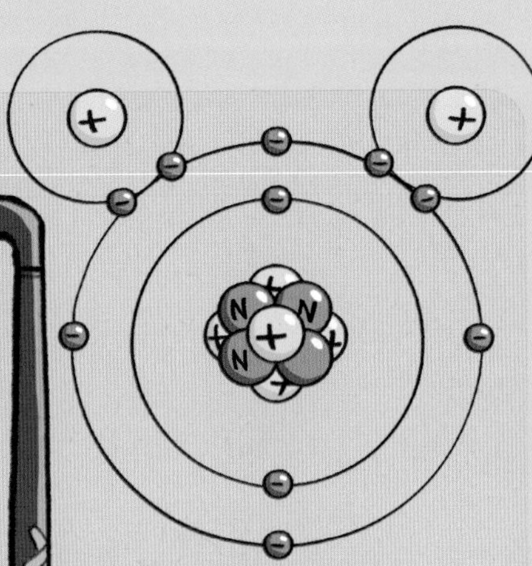

compound molecule H_2O

The most **famous** compound is probably water. Water's chemical symbol is H_2O, which shows that it is made from two hydrogen atoms (H_2) and an oxygen atom (O).

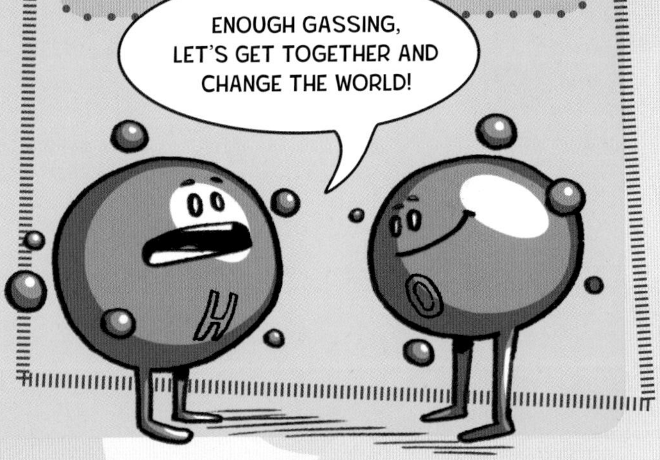

ENOUGH GASSING, LET'S GET TOGETHER AND CHANGE THE WORLD!

STATES OF MATTER

SOLID   **LIQUID**   **GAS**

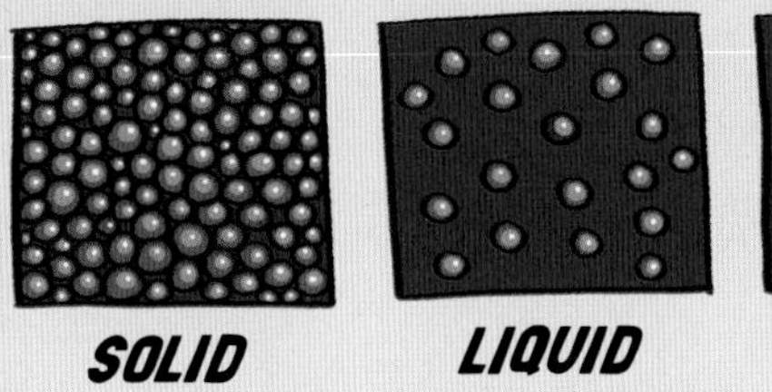

In chemistry, there are three main states of matter: **solid, liquid and gas**.

Solids are materials with a **fixed shape and size**. Their molecules are tightly packed together.

THIS IS ALSO SOMETIMES KNOWN AS 'COMMUTING'...

Liquids are substances with a **fixed volume** that change shape to match whatever container they are in. The molecules in a liquid are still tightly packed together, but they can move more than molecules in a solid.

Gases can be **any shape or volume**, as their molecules are not tightly packed together and can move around easily.

SORRY! THAT ONE MAY HAVE MOVED AROUND A BIT TOO EASILY...

POOT

Chemists originally thought that there were only **three states of matter**, but now they know there is a fourth, called **plasma**, which can be found in the interior of the Sun. The human-made version is used to create plasma television screens.

7

HYDROGEN

1 H

HYDROGEN IS THE MOST IMPORTANT ELEMENT IN THE UNIVERSE. It is the building block that all other elements and compounds rely on.

Hydrogen is the **first element** in the periodic table, with an atomic number of one.

It is the **lightest element**, with only one proton and one electron in each hydrogen atom.

Hydrogen is colourless and **odourless**.

Hydrogen is **lighter than air** and was used to fill gas balloons and airships in the earliest days of air travel.

More hydrogen exists than any other element; it makes up at least **90% of all the atoms** in the universe.

I'M NEITHER OF THOSE THINGS!

Hydrogen is **highly flammable**, meaning it catches fire easily. This led to some tragic accidents in the early days of air travel. In the Hindenburg disaster of 1937, a hydrogen-filled airship caught fire and crashed.

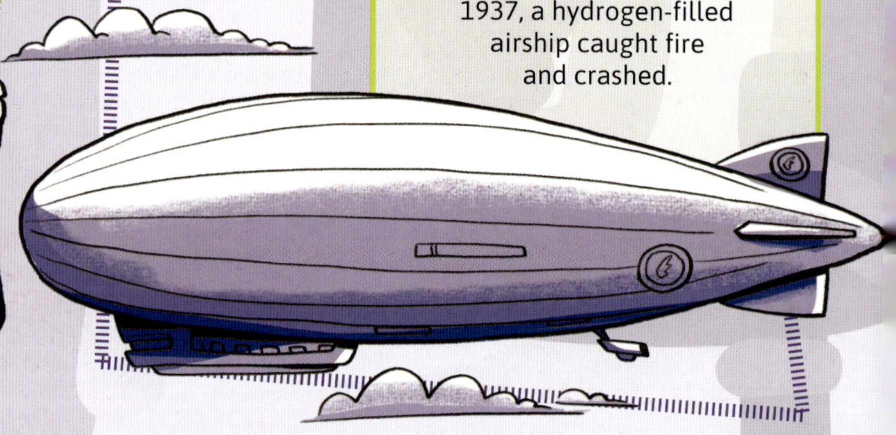

TSS TSS

Hydrogen can be used as a **clean fuel**, as it only produces water when it burns, rather than the harmful gases that are released by burning fossil fuels.

Hydrogen becomes a liquid at a very low temperature, and under extremely high pressure it can even become a **liquid metal**. It is thought that metallic hydrogen may exist naturally at the cores of gas giant planets, such as Jupiter.

THE ORIGINALS!

THE UNIVERSE'S MIGHTIEST ELEMENTS!

Hydrogen makes up about 10% of the mass of the **human body**.

Hydrogen is one of the three elements forged in the **Big Bang** that created the universe. The others were lithium and helium.

I THOUGHT HUMANS WERE FULL OF HOT AIR!

Hydrogen is the only element that can exist **without** neutrons.

Liquid hydrogen is combined with liquid oxygen to make **rocket fuel**.

I WOULDN'T WANT TO GET INTO THIS OLD RUST BUCKET!

HAVEN'T THEY HEARD OF TELEPORTATION?

On Earth, hydrogen is mostly found in **water**. Remember, it puts the 'H' in H_2O!

ALKALI METALS

Alkali metals all have low melting points. They are good conductors, which means they allow heat and electricity to pass through them easily. They are also highly reactive and are usually found in the natural world in compounds with other elements.

3 Li — LITHIUM

Lithium is a key **component** in batteries.

Lithium is created when **stars** reach the end of their lives and **explode**!

Lithium burns with such an **intense** flame that it can be very difficult to put out.

It is also **very soft** and can easily be cut with a butter knife.

LITHIUM BUTTER

11 Na — SODIUM

There is lots of sodium on Earth. It makes up **2.8%** of the planet's crust.

If your body runs low on sodium, it will cause your **muscles** to cramp.

It was discovered by Sir Humphry Davy in **1807**.

Sodium is in **salt**, which is the common name for the compound sodium chloride.

Sodium floats **on** water, but will ignite **underwater**!

I TOLD YOU A SODIUM RAFT WAS A BAD IDEA...

19 K — POTASSIUM

When potassium is added to water, it reacts **explosively**, burning with a lilac flame.

Compounds of potassium are used in **gunpowder**.

Both potassium and sodium are **solid** at room temperature. When they are combined at room temperature, they make a **liquid**.

Potassium is used in the manufacture of **fertilisers**.

COME ON, WHO NEEDS POTASSIUM TO MAKE FERTILISER WHEN YOU HAVE ME?

37 Rb RUBIDIUM

Rubidium was discovered by **Robert Bunsen** and **Gustav Kirchhoff** in 1861.

Rubidium immediately reacts with air and **catches fire**, which means that it has to be stored in oil.

It is used in **fireworks** to give the explosions a purple colour.

Rubidium has a low melting point of **39°C** (102°F), only **2°C** (4°F) warmer than the human body.

MAYBE A RUBIDIUM TEAPOT WASN'T SUCH A GOOD IDEA!

55 Cs CAESIUM

Caesium's name comes from a Latin word meaning **sky blue**.

Caesium is a metal but is **liquid** at room temperature.

It is used in the manufacture of incredibly accurate **atomic** clocks.

Large quantities of **radioactive** caesium were released into the atmosphere by the **Chernobyl nuclear accident** in 1986.

I BET YOU CAN'T USE THE WORD CAESIUM IN A SENTENCE.

IT'S EASY... UM...

Radioactive atoms emit energy and particles naturally and can sometimes be very dangerous.

87 Fr FRANCIUM

Francium is extremely radioactive. It only exists for about **20 minutes** before it decays into other elements, such as astatine, radon or radium.

Due to its intense radioactivity, francium is only really used in **scientific research**.

Francium is the second rarest natural element after astatine. **Fewer than 28g** (1oz) of francium exists on Earth at any given time.

Francium is named after France, as it was discovered in a laboratory in **Paris**.

IF IT WAS DISCOVERED IN BELGIUM, WOULD IT BE CALLED BELGIUMIUM?

11

ALKALINE-EARTH METALS

Alkaline-earth metals are the second most reactive group of elements. They are usually shiny, silvery-white metals that melt easily.

4 Be — BERYLLIUM

Beryllium is **six times** stiffer than steel.

The United States is the world's **largest producer** of beryllium.

Beryllium is not magnetic, which means it is useful for creating sensitive **radio and radar** equipment.

The mirrors in NASA's special space **telescope** are composed mostly of beryllium.

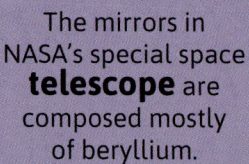

BERYLLIANT!

12 Mg — MAGNESIUM

Magnesium fires can be **highly dangerous**, as adding water to them produces hydrogen, which makes the fire burn even more fiercely.

Magnesium is very important for the human body. It helps to keep your nerves and muscles working properly and keeps your heart, bones and **immune system** strong.

Burning magnesium powder was once used to create the **flash** for photography.

Bath salts are often made of magnesium.

Earth contains enough magnesium to make a **Mars-sized planet** and three moons!

ERM...

BUT WHO NEEDS THAT AMOUNT OF BATH SALTS?

20 Ca — CALCIUM

Calcium's name comes from the **Latin** word for lime, *calx*.

The saying **being in the limelight** is a reference to the fact that lime (calcium oxide) lamps used to light up the stage in Victorian theatres.

Calcium is important for building strong **teeth and bones**. The human body contains about 1kg (2.2lb) of calcium, 99% of which is in the bones and teeth.

Calcium is **used by humans and snails** to build their homes. Humans use it to manufacture cement and concrete. Snails use it to make their shells.

BRIAN'S NOT BEEN THE SAME SINCE HE GOT INTO HOME IMPROVEMENTS...

38 Sr — STRONTIUM

Strontium is named after a village called Strontian in **Scotland**, where a rock containing the element was first found.

Strontium is very important in the treatment of **bone cancer**.

Strontium salts burn with a bright red flame, so can be used to make **fireworks** and distress flares.

It is also used to make a type of **glass** that blocks X-rays, which is important for certain kinds of medical equipment.

> WE ALIENS USE IT FOR AROMATHERAPY!

56 Ba — BARIUM

Barium is a soft, silvery metal that **turns black** when cut due to exposure to oxygen in the air.

Barium gets its name from the Greek word *barys*, meaning **heavy**.

It was discovered in the 1600s in a rock called **Bologna stone**, named after the Italian city where it was found.

Barium salts burn with a **green flame** and so, like strontium, barium is very useful in the manufacture of fireworks.

Some people have to **swallow** barium before having an X-ray, so that their digestive system can be seen.

> HUH, I DON'T NEED BARIUM TO SHOW OFF MY INSIDES!

88 Ra — RADIUM

Radium was first discovered by **Marie Curie** in 1898.

Radium was once used to produce radon gas for **cancer treatment**, but safer treatments are now available.

Radium's name comes from the Latin word *radius*, meaning 'ray', because of the **radioactive rays** it emits.

Radium was originally used in paint for **clocks and watches**, to make the hands glow in the dark. We now know that its emissions are too dangerous for day-to-day use.

TRANSITION METALS

Transition metals sit in the centre of the periodic table. They are less reactive than the alkali metals, and they tend to be tougher, with higher melting points.

21 Sc — SCANDIUM

When exposed to the air, scandium becomes **yellow or pink**.

Scandium is much more common on the Moon and **inside the Sun** than it is on Earth.

It is used in the manufacture of baseball bats, aircraft parts and high-intensity lights for **film and TV production**.

22 Ti — TITANIUM

Titanium is named after the **Titans**, who were gods from Greek mythology.

Titanium is used in the construction of **planes, ships and spacecraft**, since it is as strong as steel but almost half the weight.

OR YOU COULD USE TOOTHPASTE AS PAINT, SUN CREAM AND MAKE-UP...

Most titanium is used to make titanium dioxide, which is a **white pigment** used in paint, sun cream, make-up, paper and toothpaste.

23 V — VANADIUM

It is **highly resistant** to corrosion (being worn down) and can even withstand the effects of acid!

Vanadium was **discovered twice**! In 1801, a letter announcing its first discovery by Andrés Manuel del Río was lost in a shipwreck. It was rediscovered in 1830 by Swedish chemist Nils Sefström.

Vanadium **stays hard** at very high temperatures, so it is used in circular saws, drill bits, engine turbines and other moving parts that get really hot.

Vanadium is named after Vanadis, the Scandinavian **goddess** of beauty.

24 Cr — CHROMIUM

Using a technique called **electroplating**, a thin layer of chromium can be applied to metal and plastic objects, including car parts and household appliances, to give a shiny finish.

Chromium is the **third hardest** element, just behind carbon and boron.

Chromium has a very high melting point of **1,890°C** (3,434°F).

25 Mn — MANGANESE

There is evidence that manganese was used as a pigment in ancient **cave paintings** and that early humans used it as make-up nearly 50,000 years ago.

Manganese takes its name from the Latin word *magnes*, meaning **magnet**, even though it isn't magnetic.

It is an essential part of **photosynthesis**. Without manganese, plants would not produce oxygen.

26 Fe — IRON

Humans have been using iron to make tools and weapons since ancient times. The first iron found by humans probably came from **meteorites** – pieces of rock or metal that fall to Earth from space.

Its chemical symbol, Fe, comes from the **Latin** word for iron, *ferrum*.

Mars' **red colour** is due to the amount of iron oxide, also know as 'rust', on the planet's surface.

Animals and plants need iron. Plants use iron in photosynthesis, and humans need iron to help their **blood** carry oxygen around their bodies.

27 Co — COBALT

Cobalt is best known for its use in dyes. Cobalt blue, a bright blue pigment, was widely used in antique **Chinese porcelain**.

Cobalt gets its name from the German word *kobalt*, which means **goblin**.

In the 1960s, cobalt was added to beer, so that the beer kept its foam once poured, but it was found to be **unhealthy**!

JUST WHEN YOU THINK HUMANS CAN'T GET ANY WEIRDER...

IRON FILINGS

COBALT BEER? NO, NO, NO. COBALT MILKSHAKES ARE WHAT YOU WANT...

15

28 Ni — NICKEL

Nickel was first identified by scientists in **1751**.

The United States' five-cent coin, known as the nickel, is actually only made from **25%** nickel; the rest is copper.

Experts believe that Earth's core is made up of molten nickel and iron. Most of the nickel on Earth is deep within the core, so the nickel that humans mine has usually been left by **meteorite impacts**.

YES... METEORITES... THAT'S RIGHT. CERTAINLY NOT CRASHED ALIEN SHIPS, NO, NO, NO!

29 Cu — COPPER

Copper is **naturally antibacterial**, which is why many public buildings have door handles containing copper to reduce the spread of diseases.

The Statue of Liberty is made of copper. It used to be copper coloured, but **exposure to air** has slowly turned it green.

Small amounts of copper can be found in Earth's water supply. In a swimming pool, it is actually the copper in the water that can make blonde hair turn **slightly green**. It's nothing to do with the chlorine!

LOOK. THE SWIMMING POOL'S TURNED ZORTLFLORT'S HAIR BLONDE!

30 Zn — ZINC

Zinc is the second most common metal in the human body. It is important for **immune function**.

Zinc's name comes from the German word *zinke*, which means 'pointed'. This is due to the **pointed crystals** that form when zinc is **smelted**. Smelting is when metal is extracted from its ore (a naturally occuring mineral containing metal) by heating and melting.

Most zinc is used in the process of **galvanisation**, which uses zinc to protect other metals from corrosion.

39 Y — YTTRIUM

In 1794, Johan Gadolin isolated yttrium in the mineral ytterbite, which is **named after** the town of Ytterby in Sweden.

Yttrium is a **superconductor**, which means it can carry an electrical charge with no resistance. It is, therefore, important to the electronics industry.

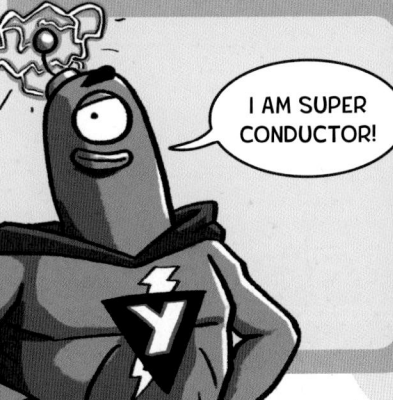

I AM SUPER CONDUCTOR!

40 Zr — ZIRCONIUM

Zirconium was discovered in Berlin in **1789** by Martin Heinrich Klaproth.

Zirconium is used in the **fuel rods** inside nuclear power stations.

It is highly flammable as a powder and **spontaneously catches fire**, burning at temperatures of **4,500°C** (8,132°F).

42 Mo — MOLYBDENUM

Molybdenum can be found much more easily on the **Moon** than on Earth.

WHAT? YOU HAVEN'T STARTED MINING ON THE MOON YET? WHAT ARE YOU WAITING FOR?

Molybdenum was used to make **Big Bertha**, the largest cannon used in World War II.

41 Nb — NIOBIUM

Niobium is named after **Niobe**, the Greek goddess of tears.

Niobium is a shiny, white metal that quickly oxidises in the air, forming a **blue-green or yellow** outer layer.

Niobium can be used to make colourful earrings and body jewellery, as it's safe to use in **body piercings**.

I SAID NO TENTACLE PIERCINGS UNTIL YOU WERE 375 YEARS OLD!

43 Tc — TECHNETIUM

Technetium is named after the **Greek word** technetos, which means 'artificial'.

Technetium can be used to reduce the corrosion of steel, but its **radioactivity** limits its uses.

Technetium was the first element to be **artificially created**. It was made by Carlo Perrier and Emilio Segrè at the University of Palermo, Sicily, in 1937.

44 Ru — RUTHENIUM

Ruthenium is a brittle, silvery-white metal that **does not rust**.

It is used to make **solar panels**.

Ruthenium is **extremely rare**. Only about 12 tonnes (13 tons) of it is mined every year!

HEY, RUTH, WHAT SHOULD WE CALL THIS ONE?

RUTH

45 Rh — RHODIUM

Rhodium is the world's **rarest precious metal**, ahead of gold or silver.

Most of the rhodium produced is used in **catalytic converters** in cars, which reduce harmful emissions by turning carbon monoxide and other gases into cleaner ones.

It is highly **resistant to corrosion** and is often used as a protective layer that adds shine to jewellery.

I LOVE MY SHINY BLING!

46 Pd — PALLADIUM

Palladium was first isolated in **1803** and was named after the **Pallas asteroid** that had just been discovered.

Palladium is used to give **white gold** its colour.

73 Ta — TANTALUM

Tantalum is named after the mythological **Greek king, Tantalus**.

Tantalum is widely used in **medical implants**, as it does not react with, or harm, living tissue.

It has the **fourth** highest melting point of the metals in the periodic table.

48 Cd — CADMIUM

Cadmium is **toxic**, but people weren't aware of this until the Industrial Revolution.

Cadmium is used in **rechargeable batteries** and as a protective coating on aeroplanes.

Cadmium **does not exist naturally**, but is produced during the production of zinc. Producing **1 tonne** (1.1 tons) of zinc only makes about **3kg** (7lb) of cadmium.

HAVE YOU FOUND IT YET?

72 Hf — HAFNIUM

Hafnium powder is **pyrophoric**, which means it will catch fire all on its own when exposed to the air.

Hafnium is used in control rods in the **reactors** powering nuclear submarines.

Hafnium carbide has the highest melting point of any two-element compound at **3,890°C** (7,034°F). That helps to explain why it's used in rocket engines!

SO, LET ME GET THIS STRAIGHT, THEY SIT IN A METAL TUBE ON TOP OF AN EXPLOSION...

47 Ag — SILVER

Silver's chemical symbol comes from the Latin word, *argentum*, which means **shining**.

Silver conducts **heat and electricity** better than any other metal.

Silver is the most **reflective** metal and is used to make mirrors and optical devices such as telescopes.

CAN I STOP DIGGING YET?

There is evidence that people mined silver as far back as **5,000 years ago**.

74 W — TUNGSTEN

Tungsten is the **strongest** of all the metals and also has the **highest melting point** at 3,422°C (6,192°F).

The glowing metal element in older **light bulbs** is made from tungsten.

Tungsten's chemical symbol comes from the element's original name, **wolfram**.

WUNGSTEN?

75 Re — RHENIUM

Rhenium is named after the Latin word for the **Rhine River** in Germany.

Rhenium is one of the rarest elements, with an average of less than one part per **billion** in Earth's crust.

It is highly heat resistant and is therefore used in the manufacture of **jet engines**.

76 Os — OSMIUM

Osmium is the **rarest** metal in Earth's crust.

Osmium is **extremely dense**. It is used in fountain pen tips and the needles of record players.

Osmium is named after the Greek word *osme*, which means **smell**.

YOU'RE VERY... ERM... OSMATIC.

WHY, THANK YOU!

77 Ir — IRIDIUM

The **Willamette Meteorite**, which was the largest meteorite to land in North America, was rich in iridium.

Iridium is the most corrosion-resistant **element** in the periodic table.

When scientists discovered an unusually large amount of iridium in a layer of clay, they concluded it was probably left by a meteorite millions of years ago. The dramatic effects of that meteorite impact might have been what caused the **extinction of the dinosaurs**.

ACTUALLY... ERM... THIS IS AWKWARD... THAT WAS US!

78 Pt — PLATINUM

Platinum is **ten times rarer** than gold and is used to make jewellery.

A cylinder of 90% platinum and 10% iridium was used as the **international standard** for measuring a kilogram until 2019.

It is hard to refine. It can take up to six months and 10 tonnes (11 tons) of ore to produce **28g** (1oz) of pure platinum.

THIS IS GOING TO TAKE FOREVER!

79 Au — GOLD

Gold is the **only metal** that is yellow or 'golden'. Other metals can turn a yellowish colour, but only if they oxidise or react with other chemicals.

Gold is the **most malleable metal**, which means that 28g (1oz) of gold could be hammered into an incredibly thin sheet measuring $17m^2$ ($183ft^2$).

There is estimated to be **9 billion tonnes** (10 billion tons) of gold in the Earth's oceans; unfortunately most of it is too difficult to extract.

I LIKE HUMANS BUT I'M ALLERGIC TO THEIR JEWELLERY...

Gold is non-toxic and **can be eaten** or drunk. You can still be allergic to it though!

80 Hg — MERCURY

Mercury is the only metal that is **liquid** at room temperature.

Mercury is highly **toxic**, but it was thought to be good for people's health for a long time.

Mercury is **not allowed** on aeroplanes because it can cause aluminium, which most planes are largely made from, to rust.

I TOLD YOU THIS WOULDN'T WORK, FREDDIE!

104 Rf — RUTHERFORDIUM

Rutherfordium is named after **Ernest Rutherford**, who is known as the founder of nuclear physics and nuclear chemistry.

It is only used for **research** purposes and has no real use in day-to-day life.

There is an ongoing argument about whether Rutherfordium was discovered by **Russian or American** scientists.

105 Db — DUBNIUM

Dubnium is named after the **Russian** town of Dubna, where it was first made.

It is extremely radioactive and is a **synthetic or human-made** element that is only used for research purposes.

HELLO! I'M SNORTLEBUZZ THE WEIRD ELEMENT HUNTER! I ONLY LIKE RARE AND UNUSUAL ELEMENTS AND THERE ARE SOME GREAT EXAMPLES ON THESE PAGES!

106 Sg — SEABORGIUM

Only a few atoms of seaborgium have been produced in laboratories. Scientists think it is a metal, but its physical properties are **impossible** to determine for now.

The periodic table's inventor, Dmitri Mendeleev predicted that seaborgium would exist. He called the element **eka-tungsten** because of its location near tungsten in the periodic table.

Seaborgium is named after Nobel Prize winner Glenn Seaborg. It was discovered in **1974**.

NO, NO I'M GLENN CYBORG...

107 Bh — BOHRIUM

Bohrium was discovered in 1976 and is named after **Niels Bohr**, who is famous for his work in quantum mechanics (a study of the physics of very small things, such as atoms and electrons).

Bohrium is a synthetic radioactive element. **Only a few atoms** have ever been produced in laboratories.

Bohrium is very radioactive. Its most stable form only lasts for **40 seconds**.

108 Hs — HASSIUM

Hassium **decays so quickly** that scientists doubt they will ever be able to make an amount large enough to properly study.

Hassium is named after the central German state of **Hesse**.

The first sample of hassium was created by a nuclear reaction that **fused lead with iron**. Since then, only a handful of atoms of hassium have been created.

109 Mt — MEITNERIUM

This element was discovered at the Heavy Ion Laboratory in Darmstadt, Germany, in **1982**.

Meitnerium is named after scientist **Lise Meitner**. She was an Austrian-Swedish physicist who contributed to the discoveries of the element protactinium and **nuclear fission** (a process that produces huge amounts of energy by splitting a nucleus into two parts).

Only small amounts of meitnerium have ever been made and it is only used in **scientific study**.

THE RARER THE BETTER FOR ME!

110 Ds — DARMSTADTIUM

Darmstadtium is named after the city where it was first made, **Darmstadt**.

It was only discovered in **1994**.

Darmstadtium is made when **nickel and lead** atoms are fused at a specific high speed.

111 Rg — ROENTGENIUM

Roentgenium only exists for **23 seconds** before it decays into other elements, which makes it very tricky to study.

Roentgenium is produced artificially and was first made in **1994**.

It is named after **Wilhelm Roentgen**, who discovered the X-ray.

'TRICKY TO STUDY,' YOU SAY? JUST MY THING!

112 Cn — COPERNICIUM

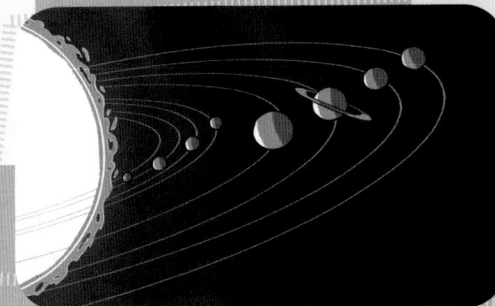

Copernicium is named after Nicolaus Copernicus, the scientist who proved that the Sun is the **centre of the solar system**, not Earth, as was commonly believed at the time.

Copernicium was discovered after a sample of lead was **pelted with zinc particles** travelling at 30kmps (19mps) for two weeks.

TWO WEEKS AT 30KMPS AND THEN SERVE IMMEDIATELY...

It is made through the fusing of **lead and zinc** atoms.

BASE METALS

Base metals are common, inexpensive, non-precious metals that tarnish, oxidise or corrode easily.

13 Al

ALUMINIUM

Aluminium is **light and strong**, which makes it the perfect material for building aircraft and spacecraft.

In the mid 19th century, aluminium was considered a precious metal. The famous French military leader Napoleon Bonaparte gave his most important dinner guests **aluminium cutlery**, as it was considered to be the height of luxury!

The efficient recycling of aluminium means that almost **75% of all aluminium** that has ever been produced is still in circulation.

Aluminium is the **third most common** element in Earth's crust and is the most common metal.

HI, I'M ALUMINIUM BUT YOU CAN CALL ME AL...

81 Tl

THALLIUM

Thallium is highly poisonous and was used historically as a **murder weapon**, earning it the nickname 'inheritance powder'.

Thallium was discovered by Sir William Crookes in London in **1861**.

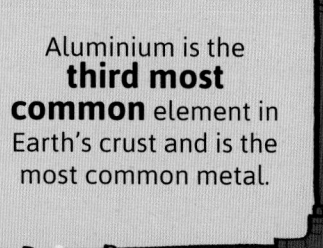

It was once used as **rat and insect poison** before its danger to humans was properly understood.

49 In — INDIUM

Indium is vital to the manufacture of **LEDs and flat-screen displays**.

Indium can be used to make **mirrors** that tarnish more slowly than mirrors made from silver.

When indium is bent, it gives off a weird **high-pitched screech**.

EEEEEK!!

THIS MIRROR MUST BE MADE OF INDIUM – IT SCREECHES EVERY TIME I LOOK INTO IT...

50 Sn — TIN

Bending a bar of tin produces a squealing sound, known as a **tin cry**.

'Sn' is tin's symbol – this comes from the Latin word for tin, which is *stannum*. *Stannum* literally means **to drip** and is probably a reference to tin's low melting point.

The gleaming gold statuettes handed out at the Oscars are actually **90% tin**!

Tin is one of the earliest metals used by humans. Archaeologists have found tools containing tin that were made **3,500 years ago**.

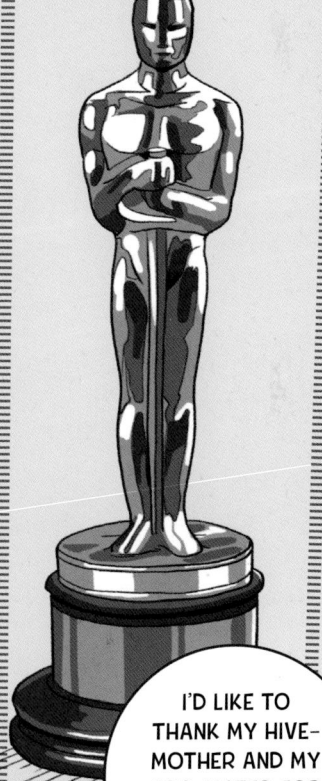

I'D LIKE TO THANK MY HIVE-MOTHER AND MY EGG-MATES FOR MAKING THIS POSSIBLE...

31 Ga — GALLIUM

Gallium is used in the **manufacture** of many modern electronic devices.

Gallium's low melting point of **29.7°C** (85.5°F), means it would melt in the palm of your hand.

Gallium has a very high boiling point, which means that it is perfect for use in **thermometers** that measure very high temperatures.

AND I THOUGHT CHOCOLATE COINS WERE USELESS...

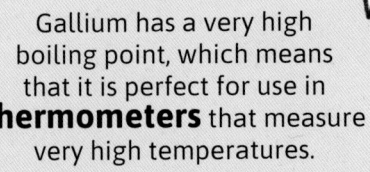

LEAD

On the planet Venus, the surface temperature is so hot (463°C / 865°F) that it can **rain lead**!

Lead was used by prehistoric humans – lead tools have been found from as far back as **4000BCE**!

Lead's chemical symbol comes from the Latin word *plumbum*, which means **waterworks**, because the Romans made water pipes out of lead.

THEY DID SAY TO EXPECT HEAVY SHOWERS TODAY...

Lead is highly effective at **blocking radiation** and is used as a lining in nuclear reactors.

The Romans used a lot of lead in their society before anyone knew how toxic it was. Most Roman citizens were probably suffering from some degree of **lead poisoning**.

BISMUTH

Bismuth has the highest **electrical resistance** of any of the elements.

Bismuth was **mistaken for lead or tin** for a long time, and was only proved to be a different metal in the 18th century.

DRIED FRUIT?

NO THANKS, I CAN'T STAND CURRENTS...

When liquid bismuth freezes, it is one of the few elements that **expands rather than contracts**, because it forms a crystalline structure similar to water.

113 Nh — NIHONIUM

Nihonium's name comes from the Japanese word for **Japan**, Nihon.

Nihonium was discovered in 2004 at the RIKEN Institute in Japan. Scientists put zinc particles in a machine called a particle accelerator, which makes particles move very quickly. When those particles reached **10% of the speed of light**, the scientists smashed them into a target made of bismuth and created nihonium.

114 Fl — FLEROVIUM

Flerovium was discovered in 1999 and it took a **40-day-long experiment** to make a single atom of the element.

Flerovium is named after **Georgy Flerov**, who founded the laboratory where it was first created.

115 Mc — MOSCOVIUM

Only discovered in **2010**, moscovium is a **synthetic radioactive metal** and has only been produced in tiny amounts.

Moscovium takes its name from **Moscow**, as it was first created in a laboratory near the Russian capital.

THESE FOUR SOUND LIKE MY KIND OF THING...

116 Lv — LIVERMORIUM

Livermorium is named after the **Lawrence Livermore National Laboratory**, which assisted in its production.

It was first made in 2000 in a year-long experiment that produced two atoms of the element. The first atom existed for about a **tenth of a second**.

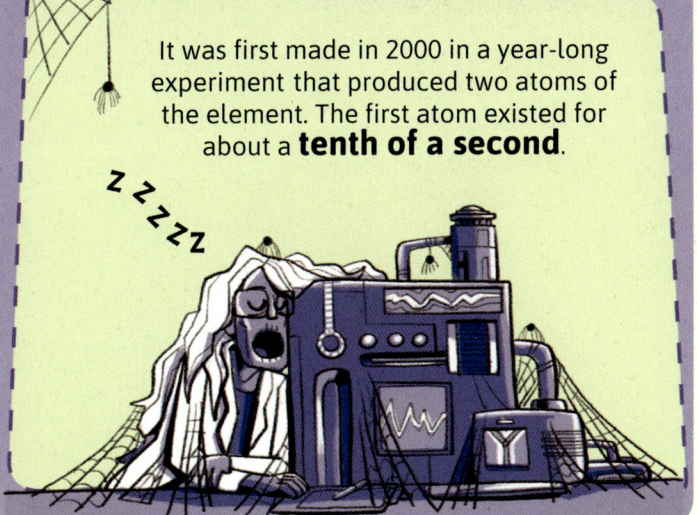

METALLOIDS

Metalloids are elements that still have a shiny metallic appearance but are more brittle than true metals.

5 B — BORON

THAT'S ONE WAY TO DO IT!

Plants need boron to help strengthen their cell walls.

Boron is the second hardest element and has a very **high melting and boiling point**.

Boron fibres are used as a structural material in **aircraft and spacecraft**.

14 Si — SILICON

Silicon is everywhere! It's the **second most common element** in Earth's crust and silicon dioxide (sand) is the most commonly found compound.

Silicon Valley, an area in the United States where lots of technology companies are based, is named after silicon, due to its importance in the manufacture of electronic devices.

Some of the earliest tools made by humans included sharp flints made from silica – the mineral silicon is extracted from. These included **Stone Age hunting tools** and woodworking tools.

32 Ge — GERMANIUM

Germanium was the first element to be named after a country, **Germany**.

Germanium was an unknown element when Dmitri Mendeleev created the periodic table. He **predicted its existence** though and suggested how it might behave. His predictions were very close to what was later discovered.

33 As — ARSENIC

Throughout history, arsenic was one of the most commonly used **poisons**. It also crops up in lots of murder mystery books! It's fairly easy to detect, though, as traces of arsenic will be present in hair, blood and urine.

Despite being poisonous, arsenic can be **good** for your health! Tiny amounts are important in the diets of chickens, goats, rodents and possibly even humans.

I DON'T UNDERSTAND WHY OUR NEW HEALTH FOOD WITH ADDED ARSENIC HASN'T BEEN MORE POPULAR WITH THE HUMANS...

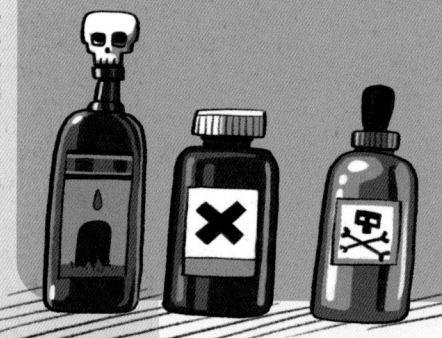

34 Se — SELENIUM

Selenium is named after **Selene**, the mythological Greek goddess of the Moon.

Brazil nuts are high in selenium. A single nut provides enough selenium to meet the daily requirement for a human adult.

Selenium salts are used to help control **dandruff**, and selenium can be used to treat mercury poisoning.

BUT I DON'T HAVE MERCURY POISONING...

51 Sb — ANTIMONY

I LOVE THIS NEW EYE-LINER!

The ancient Egyptians used the mineral form of antimony to make kohl, a black **eye make-up**.

Antimony has been used for thousands of years. The Louvre Museum in France contains an **ancient vase** made of antimony.

Antimony is not malleable but **hard and brittle**, and can be crushed down to a powder. Antimony is also a poor conductor of electricity and heat.

52 Te — TELLURIUM

Exposure to tellurium can cause health problems and can even make your breath **smell of garlic**!

Tellurium's main use is making **photovoltaic cells** for solar panels.

Tellurium has been detected in **space**, but it is very rare on Earth – eight times rarer than gold, in fact!

84 Po — POLONIUM

Marie and Pierre Curie discovered polonium in **1898**. Marie Curie named polonium after her homeland, Poland.

TASTES OF MINT...

Po

Polonium is **highly toxic**. The first person to die of polonium poisoning may have been Marie Curie's daughter, Irène Joliot-Curie. In 1946, a capsule of polonium **exploded** on her lab bench. This may have caused her death from leukaemia, a type of cancer, ten years later.

Polonium and beryllium were used in the trigger of the **first atomic bomb**. Once mixed, the two elements set off the explosion.

NON-METALS

Non-metals are elements that do not have any of the properties of metals. They don't look metallic, they can't be stretched or shaped and they are poor conductors of heat and electricity. Hydrogen is technically a non-metal too, but it has its own spot on the periodic table because it has to be different!

6
C

CARBON

Carbon occurs in **all living things**.

It can take the form of one of the hardest substances, **diamond**, or one of the softest, **graphite**.

IT CAN BE OVER 18%, BUT ONLY IF YOU LEAVE THEM IN THE OVEN FOR TOO LONG...

Carbon makes up **18%** of the total mass of the human body.

LE CHEF

Fossil fuels were once living things, so they contain a lot of carbon. When they are burnt, this carbon is released as the gas **carbon dioxide**, which is one of the main contributors to **global warming**.

Carbon has the **highest melting point** of all the elements. The melting point of diamond is approximately **3,550°C** (6,442°F)!

8
O

OXYGEN

Oxygen makes up two thirds of the weight of **all living things**! This is because water is the heaviest part of living things, and oxygen and hydrogen make water.

When in its liquid form, oxygen is **pale blue**. It's also attracted to magnets!

Plants make oxygen through the process of photosynthesis. Without living things, there would be no oxygen. So, if we find other planets with oxygen in their atmospheres, this would be a good indication of **extraterrestrial life**!

It does not burn! Oxygen is good at helping other things to burn, but it is not flammable itself. This is for the best, really, as otherwise lighting a match would ignite all of the oxygen in the atmosphere.

METHANE IN THE ATMOSPHERE IS ANOTHER INDICATOR OF LIFE, BUT THAT'S FORMED BY A DIFFERENT CHEMICAL PROCESS...

EXCUSE ME!

NITROGEN

Nitrogen becomes a liquid at a temperature of **-196°C** (-320°F), which is pretty cold! It's really useful in this form as a coolant in electronics and **medical procedures**.

About **78% of Earth's atmosphere** is made up of nitrogen. That's nothing compared to Titan, one of Saturn's moons, whose atmosphere is 98% nitrogen!

Nitrogen can be bad for **scuba divers** though! If divers surface too quickly, this can cause nitrogen bubbles to form in their blood. This is an extremely painful and sometimes fatal condition called **the bends**.

Nitrogen was once called **burnt air** because air with the oxygen removed is almost entirely made up of nitrogen.

IT'S NOT BURNT, IT'S CARAMELISED...

LE CHEF

PHOSPHORUS

Phosphorus was accidentally discovered in **1669** by an alchemist called Hennig Brand. He was heating **urine** in an attempt to make a substance that could create gold.

THAT'S THE LAST TIME I LET HENNIG MAKE ME A CUP OF TEA...

Brand named the element after the Greek word *phosphoros*, which means **bringer of light**.

Phosphorus earnt the nickname **the devil's element** due to the fact that it emits a weird green glow, sometimes bursts into flames and was the thirteenth element discovered.

SULFUR

Sulfur can be found around volcano vents. It used to be called 'brimstone', which means **stone that burns**.

When sulfur is burnt, usually as a result of fossil fuel production, it produces sulfur dioxide, which is the main ingredient of **acid rain**.

When sulfur mixes with iron, it produces a worthless substance called **iron pyrite**. This looks so much like gold that it is known as **fool's gold**.

Sulfur is associated with some very bad smells. It contributes to the **pungent aromas** of rotten eggs, onions, garlic and skunks' spray.

MAYBE I SHOULD REDUCE THE AMOUNT OF SULFUR IN MY DIET...

HALOGENS

Halogens are a group of non-metallic elements that cover all the physical states of matter. At room temperature, fluorine and chlorine are gases, bromine is a liquid and iodine is a solid.

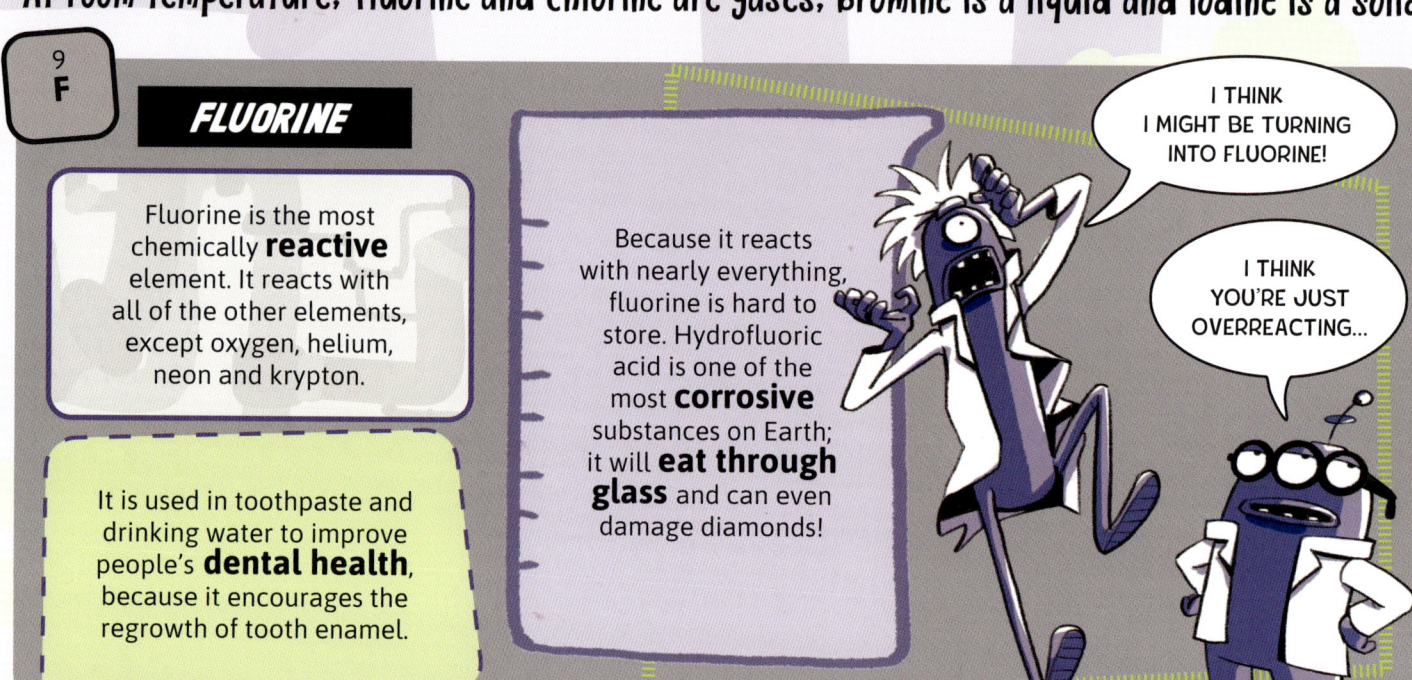

9 F

FLUORINE

Fluorine is the most chemically **reactive** element. It reacts with all of the other elements, except oxygen, helium, neon and krypton.

It is used in toothpaste and drinking water to improve people's **dental health**, because it encourages the regrowth of tooth enamel.

Because it reacts with nearly everything, fluorine is hard to store. Hydrofluoric acid is one of the most **corrosive** substances on Earth; it will **eat through glass** and can even damage diamonds!

I THINK I MIGHT BE TURNING INTO FLUORINE!

I THINK YOU'RE JUST OVERREACTING...

17 Cl

CHLORINE

In its natural gas state, chlorine is **extremely dangerous**. Breathing in air that is only 0.1% chlorine could be fatal!

The most well-known compound of chlorine is **sodium chloride**, or salt. There is so much chlorine stored in salty seawater that if all of it was released at once, it would produce **three times more gas** than Earth's atmosphere.

I TOO CAN PRODUCE THREE TIMES MORE GAS THAN EARTH'S ATMOSPHERE!

Small amounts of liquefied chlorine are used to make **drinking water safe** as it is a disinfectant.

GAS

35 Br — BROMINE

Bromine is the only non-metal that is a **liquid** at room temperature.

Bromine is a reddish-brown liquid that evaporates into a red gas with a **strong odour** similar to chlorine. This smell gives bromine its name, after the Greek word *bromos*, which means 'stench'.

Bromine was discovered in 1826 by two scientists working independently – **Antoine Balard and Carl Löwig**. Unfortunately Löwig was a schoolboy at the time of the discovery and couldn't publish his findings, leaving Balard to get the credit!

53 I — IODINE

Radioactive iodine can both **cause and treat** cancer.

The human body needs iodine to help regulate its **metabolism**, which is the speed at which the body's natural processes work. Most of the iodine in an average person's diet comes from **milk or cheese**, because it is in the grass that cows eat.

In **1839**, Louis Daguerre, a French painter, put liquid iodine on a silver-coated copper plate, and exposed the plate to light. This was the first **true photograph**, though at the time it was called a 'daguerreotype' after its creator.

THE FIRST SELFIE WAS TAKEN TWO HOURS LATER...

85 At — ASTATINE

Astatine is the **rarest element** on Earth. It is estimated that there are only about **25 grams** (1oz) of naturally occurring astatine in Earth's crust at any given time.

Astatine cannot be seen with the naked eye, since a large enough sample would almost **instantly disintegrate** because of its own radioactivity. This helps to explain its name, which is taken from the Greek word *astatos*, meaning 'unstable'.

117 Ts — TENNESSINE

Tennessine was first created in **2010** in a particle accelerator. Two atoms were created and neither of them existed for more than a tenth of a second.

The element is named after the state **Tennessee** in the United States.

NOBLE GASES

The noble gases, which are sometimes called 'inert gases', are the least reactive elements in the periodic table.

2 He — HELIUM

Helium was discovered in the Sun's atmosphere before it was found on Earth, so it was named after **Helios**, the Greek god of the Sun.

When helium is cooled to very low temperatures, it turns from a gas into a liquid with a very weird property called **superfluidity**. A superfluid has no friction and can climb up and over the sides of any open container it's stored in!

Helium is the second most common element in the universe – there's not much on Earth, but there's **lots in stars**.

Helium is so light that it ignores the effects of **Earth's gravity**. Helium released at ground level will eventually escape into space.

WHO NEEDS ROCKETS?

18 Ar — ARGON

Argon was the first noble gas to be discovered and is the **third most common gas** on Earth, making up about 1.3% of the atmosphere.

Argon is used in metal welding and **wine-making**.

Important historical documents are stored in sealed, argon-filled glass cases to **prevent decay**.

WHAT'S SO IMPORTANT ABOUT A CERAMIC ARTIST CALLED HARRY?

10 Ne — NEON

Neon is common in the universe, but it's harder to find on Earth. It is produced when air is compressed. The process is not efficient though, as it takes about **40 tonnes** (44 tons) of liquid air to make 0.5kg (1lb) of neon.

It is commonly used in neon signs, but neon itself only **glows with a red colour**. The other colours in so-called neon signs are produced by different gases, such as argon, helium, krypton and xenon.

Neon's name comes from the Greek word *neos*, which means '**new**'.

36 Kr — KRYPTON

Krypton is a colourless gas and should **not be confused** with a green crystal that can hurt Superman...

Krypton was discovered partially by accident in **1898**, which is why it is named after the Greek word *krypto*, meaning 'hidden'.

Krypton is used in some of the most **powerful lasers** in the world. A krypton-fluorine laser can produce a pulse of energy 500 times as strong as the entire United States electrical grid in just **four-billionths of a second**!

CHASE THE LASER, KITTY!

54 Xe — XENON

Most people know that inhaling helium from a balloon can make your voice high-pitched and squeaky, but did you know that if you inhale xenon it can **make your voice deeper**?

In the future, xenon may help humans to explore the universe. NASA engineers are experimenting with ways they could use xenon to **propel spacecraft** on deep space missions.

HUMANS? IN DEEP SPACE? HA! THAT'LL BE THE DAY...

Electric lights made using xenon are **extremely bright**. They are used for things such as powerful car headlights and floodlights, which need to illuminate things at night.

86 Rn — RADON

Radon is the **heaviest** known gas. It's over seven times heavier than air.

Radon gas is colourless, but it emits a **brilliant yellow light** when it freezes.

Radon is **radioactive** and can cause cancer if exposure levels are too high. In the past, miners often suffered from a disease known then as *mala metallorum*, which translates from Latin as 'bad metals'. This was later discovered to be **lung cancer**, caused by the high levels of radon found in deep mines.

118 Og — OGANESSON

Oganesson was discovered in **2002** when a sample of calcium was bombarded with californium atoms in a particle accelerator for **45 days**. That produced just two atoms of oganesson, which existed for less than **three milliseconds**!

TWO ATOMS? THAT'S FAR TOO COMMON FOR ME...

35

RARE EARTHS

Rare earths are silver, silvery-white or grey metals that tarnish if exposed to the air and have high electrical conductivity. Rare earths generally are not very 'rare', but they are called this because they are less common than other metals.

57 La — LANTHANUM

Lanthanum compounds are used in the flints of lighters, electron microscopes and powerful lights used during **film production**.

I GIVE YOU LANTHANUM!

NO FLOXXLENORT, THAT'S A CHRYSANTHEMUM...

Lanthanum is a silvery-white, soft metal and is the **second most reactive** rare-earth metal.

It is also used in rechargeable batteries for **hybrid cars**.

58 Ce — CERIUM

Cerium is the most **common** rare-earth metal.

The main use for cerium is in **catalytic converters** for cars, which help to remove harmful substances in exhaust gases and protect the atmosphere.

It was named by Jöns Jakob Berzelius in **1803** after Ceres, a dwarf planet that had been discovered two years earlier.

DOESN'T HELP WITH THE HARMFUL SUBSTANCES IN OUR GASES THOUGH!

59 Pr — PRASEODYAMIUM

Throughout history, praseodymium has mainly been used as a yellow colouring for **glass and pottery**. More recently, it has been used in aircraft manufacture.

Praseodymium is named after *prasios*, the Greek word for green, as it slowly forms a **green coating** when exposed to oxygen in the air.

36

60 Nd — NEODYMIUM

Neodymium, when alloyed with iron and boron, produces the **strongest magnets** known to exist. A neodymium magnet can lift a thousand times its own weight!

Nd

Fe

OH IRON, I FEEL STRANGELY DRAWN TO YOU…

It is used as a crystal in **lasers** for treating skin cancers and to cut and weld steel.

Neodymium's name comes from the Greek phrase for **new twin**, as it is very similar in appearance to lanthanum.

61 Pm — PROMETHIUM

Promethium is the only **radioactive** rare-earth metal.

Promethium is mostly used for research, but it does have some **practical uses**, such as the manufacture of small nuclear batteries.

It is not found naturally on Earth, but it has been detected in stars hundreds of **light years** away.

62 Sm — SAMARIUM

Samarium was discovered in **1879** by French chemist Paul-Émile Lecoq de Boisbaudran.

It is used to make lights for the **film industry** and in the treatment of some cancers.

Samarium is also used in the **ceramics and electronics** industries.

63 Eu — EUROPIUM

It is named after the continent of Europe. Appropriately, it is now used in **anti-forgery marks** on Euro banknotes.

Europium is the most reactive of the rare-earth metals. It will ignite if the air temperature is above **150°C** (302°F).

WHAT DID ONE CONTINENT SAY TO THE OTHER CONTINENT FIRST THING IN THE MORNING?

I DON'T KNOW.

EUROPE EARLY TODAY!

64 Gd — GADOLINIUM

Gadolinium is very good at **absorbing neutrons**, so it is used in emergency shutdown systems of nuclear reactors.

Gadolinium can be more **magnetic** than iron, but only at low temperatures.

65 Tb — TERBIUM

NASA uses terbium to check for bacteria on its space probes to make sure that no earthly **microorganisms** hitch a ride into space.

Alloys of terbium are a vital part of the **magnets** inside modern electric motors.

Terbium is one of four elements named after the small **Swedish village** of Ytterby. The others are erbium, yttrium and ytterbium. Thulium, gadolinium and holmium were also first found there, so Ytterby is actually one of the most **important places** on the planet for the periodic table!

THANK GOODNESS FOR TERBIUM! WE DON'T WANT ANY OF YOUR HORRIBLE HUMAN GERMS, THANK YOU VERY MUCH!

YTTERBY

66 Dy — DYSPROSIUM

Paul-Émile Lecoq de Boisbaudran identified dysprosium in **1886**. It took more than 30 attempts for him to successfully isolate it, which explains the element's name. It comes from the Greek word *dysprositos*, which means **hard to get**.

Dysprosium is used in nuclear control rods, **data storage** and magnets.

67 Ho — HOLMIUM

Holmium has the **highest magnetic strength** of any element.

Holmium is used in the manufacture of **medical lasers**, nuclear control rods and super powerful magnets.

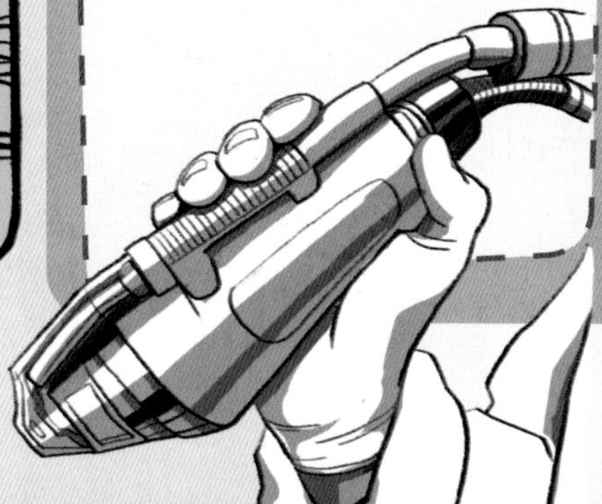

Holmium was discovered in **1878** by Swiss chemists Marc Delafontaine and Jacques-Louis Soret. They originally named their new discovery **Element X**.

I GIVE YOU... ELEMENT X!

ISN'T THAT HOLMIUM?

JUST HUMOUR HIM...

68 Er — ERBIUM

Erbium can be used in alloys to make them more **flexible** and easier to work with.

Erbium is also used to give glass or ceramics a **pink colour**.

69 Tm — THULIUM

The main source of thulium is the mineral monazite, which contains thulium at a concentration of only about **20 parts per million**.

Thulium is the **rarest** of the rare earths.

Thulium will **catch fire** at a lower temperature than paper.

Thulium is named after Thule, which was the early name for **Scandinavia**.

70 Yb — YTTERBIUM

Ytterbium is used in portable X-ray machines that **don't need electricity** to function.

Ytterbium is also used in devices that monitor the power of **earthquakes** and underground explosions.

Like many of the rare earths, ytterbium was first discovered in minerals extracted from a **single small quarry** in Ytterby.

71 Lu — LUTETIUM

Lutetium atoms are the **smallest** of any of the rare earths. That small size means lutetium also has the highest melting point, the highest density and is the hardest of all the rare earths.

It is one of the most **expensive** rare-earth metals, costing approximately £7,750 ($10,000) per kilogram. This expense, along with the difficulty of extraction, means that there aren't many uses for it.

YOU HAD TO DROP THE LUTETIUM ATOM DIDN'T YOU?

WAS THAT AN EARTHQUAKE?

YES, AN EARTHQUAKE, THAT'S IT...

RADIOACTIVE RARE EARTHS

Radioactive rare earths are a group of rare earths that are highly radioactive (the clue is in the name!).

89 Ac — ACTINIUM

A tonne (1.1 tons) of uranium ore will produce **less than 1mg** (0.0004oz) of actinium. This rarity and its intense radioactivity mean that actinium is only really used in scientific research.

Actinium is so radioactive (150 times more radioactive than radium) that it **glows blue** in the dark.

I'VE BEEN RESEARCHING ACTINIUM MY WHOLE LIFE – IT'S NEVER DONE ME ANY HARM!

92 U — URANIUM

Uranium is the **heaviest** naturally occurring element in the universe.

A uranium bomb was detonated over the Japanese city of **Hiroshima** on 6th August 1945.

Uranium was first discovered in **1789**, but it was not understood to be radioactive until **107 years later**.

90 Th — THORIUM

Thorium is created in the core of a supernova – a type of star – and then **scattered** across the galaxy when the supernova explodes.

When it's a liquid, thorium has a greater temperature range than any other element, with nearly **3,000°C** (5,500°F) between its melting and boiling points.

Extensive research is being done into using thorium in **nuclear reactors** instead of uranium. This would be good because thorium is easier to find, cheaper and less radioactive than uranium.

THOR-Y?

UM?

91 Pa — PROTACTINIUM

Protactinium is so **toxic** and so **radioactive** that it can only be used in scientific research.

Protactinium can be extracted from uranium ore but only in tiny amounts. In **1959**, it cost **$500,000** to extract 125g (4oz) from 60 tonnes (66 tons) of nuclear waste.

93 Np — NEPTUNIUM

Neptunium is not only highly radioactive but also **pyrophoric**, which means that it can **spontaneously catch fire** at room temperature.

Its name is derived from the **planet Neptune**, the next planet out from the Sun after Uranus, in the same way that neptunium is the next element in the periodic table after uranium.

There is research underway that may see neptunium being used in portable nuclear reactors on board the **spacecraft of the future**.

RIDICULOUS! EVERYBODY KNOWS THAT SPACESHIPS ARE POWERED BY A HOOPLENOXIAN FLUX CONVERTER!

94 Pu — PLUTONIUM

Plutonium has been used in nuclear weapons, including the bomb that was dropped on the Japanese city of **Nagasaki** at the end of World War II.

It is not a good conductor of electricity or heat, unlike some metals. It is also the only **radioactive** rare-earth metal that is not magnetic.

Plutonium is named after the **dwarf planet Pluto** and so follows the trend of uranium and neptunium being named for planets outwards from the Sun.

95 Am — AMERICIUM

Researchers originally called this new element **pandemonium** as a joke, because it was so hard to isolate it from curium. It was eventually named after America, because it sits below europium on the periodic table.

Like neptunium, americium is being researched as a **power source** for future spacecraft.

SO, LET ME GET THIS STRAIGHT, HUMANS ARE GOING TO TRAVEL THROUGH SPACE ON SMOKE DETECTORS?

Many **smoke detectors** contain americium.

96 Cm — CURIUM

Curium is highly radioactive and it **glows red** in the dark.

It is named after **Marie Curie** and her husband, Pierre Curie, who were pioneers in understanding radioactivity.

PANDEMONIUM AND DELIRIUM, HOW VERY HUMAN...

When scientists first discovered curium, they jokingly named it **delirium** after the trouble they had isolating it from americium.

97 Bk — BERKELIUM

Since **1967**, just over **1g** (0.03oz) of berkelium has been produced each year.

Berkelium was first isolated in 1949. It was named after **Berkeley, California**, as it was discovered at the University of California, Berkeley.

Such a **small quantity** of this element has been produced that very little is known about its properties.

ONE GRAM EVERY YEAR! NOW WE'RE TALKING!

98 Cf — CALIFORNIUM

Californium is a **radioactive** element which is not found in nature.

Californium is generated in **particle accelerators** and nuclear reactors.

It is named after **California**, since it was also discovered at the University of California, Berkeley.

Californium can be used to start up nuclear reactors, treat cancer and detect gold, silver, explosives or corrosion in aeroplanes.

99 Es — EINSTEINIUM

Einsteinium was given its name **in recognition** of Albert Einstein's massive contribution to science.

Einsteinium was discovered in debris from the **first large hydrogen bomb test**, which took place over the Pacific Ocean on 1st November 1952. Its discovery was kept secret on the orders of the military for three years.

KEPT SECRET YOU SAY, TELL ME MORE...

100 Fm — FERMIUM

Fermium was discovered in the debris of the same **hydrogen bomb test** that first produced einsteinium. It was identified in coral deposits taken from the test site.

Fermium was named in recognition of the Italian physicist and **Nobel Prize** winner Enrico Fermi, who developed the first working nuclear reactor.

102 No — NOBELIUM

It is named after **Alfred Nobel**, the inventor of dynamite and founder of the Nobel Prize.

If enough nobelium was made that **could be seen**, it would pose a severe radiation risk.

Such a tiny amount of nobelium has been produced that **no one knows what it looks like**. Researchers believe, due to its position in the periodic table, that it would be a silvery-white colour if enough could be produced to be visible.

UNKNOWN APPEARANCE? SEVERE RADIATION DANGER? THIS JUST GETS BETTER AND BETTER!

101 Md — MENDELEVIUM

It is a highly radioactive, synthetic metal and has only been produced in **tiny amounts** in laboratories.

Mendelevium is named after Mendeleev, the **creator** of the periodic table.

Mendelevium was the first element to be produced **one atom** at a time.

103 Lr — LAWRENCIUM

Lawrencium does **not occur naturally**. It is formed when curium and boron are combined in a particle accelerator.

Lawrencium is named after Ernest Lawrence, inventor of the **cyclotron particle accelerator**, which was a piece of scientific equipment vital in the discovery of many other elements.

KEEP PEDALLING!

IS THE PARTICLE GOING FAST ENOUGH YET?

NEARLY...

Lawrencium was made in **1961** by Albert Ghiorso, Torbjørn Sikkeland, Almon Larsh and Robert Latimer at the Lawrence Berkeley National Laboratory in California.

TOP TEN WEIRD FACTS

10 It's likely more elements will be added to the periodic table, but scientists predict that it will end at **137 elements**. This is because it would be scientifically impossible for elements to exist beyond that point, as their particles would have to move faster than the speed of light.

9 Dmitri Mendeleev **denied** the existence of **argon** even after it was discovered, because it didn't fit the properties that his periodic table said it should have.

> BUT DMITRI, I'M STANDING RIGHT HERE!

> Ar

8 The only letter **not to appear** in the English periodic table is 'J'.

> I GIVE YOU JABBERWOCKIUM!

> JEESH!

7 The International Union of Pure Applied Chemistry (IUPAC) is responsible for **maintaining and updating** the periodic table when new discoveries are made. The most recent revision of the periodic table was published in December 2018.

> SO, JABBERWOCKIUM GOES HERE BETWEEN UNOBTAINIUM AND DILITHIUM...

6 Every hydrogen atom in your body is **13.5 billion years old**, as every one of them was created at the birth of the universe during the Big Bang.

AGE?

UP TO 13.5 BILLION YEARS...

5 Bromine and mercury are the only elements that are liquid at **room temperature**.

3 The famous chemist Glenn Seaborg is the only person who could have given his **precise location** using the periodic table. In America (americium) you could find California (californium) and in California you could find the city of Berkeley (berkelium). In Berkeley you could find the Lawrence Berkeley National Laboratory (lawrencium), and in that laboratory you would find Glenn Seaborg (seaborgium)!

4 Atoms of an element do not necessarily get larger as their atomic number increases; element atoms usually decrease in size as you move from **left to right** across the periodic table.

2 Dmitri Mendeleev loved **card games**, which is why he wrote the atomic weight of each element on index cards and then organised them in a similar fashion to the card game solitaire.

HE WOULD HAVE LOVED MINESWEEPER!

1 If you were able to extract all the elements in your body, they would have a **current market value** of £0.80 ($1)!

I JUST FEEL SO WORTHLESS...

45

PERIODIC TABLE ACTIVITIES

Use your knowledge of the periodic table to complete these activities!

Weird Word Search

There are ten tricky elements hidden in this word search! See how many you can find...
(Answers on page 48.)

GOLD	CURIUM
SODIUM	NEON
COBALT	ARSENIC
SILICON	LEAD
OXYGEN	CARBON

S	A	R	S	E	N	I	C	I	O	B	C
Y	C	O	R	S	D	L	O	G	R	B	F
M	E	X	I	X	I	C	T	A	H	R	E
S	A	Y	C	C	S	L	L	E	A	D	C
O	F	G	R	C	U	R	I	U	M	A	N
D	T	E	Y	D	T	G	F	C	R	H	E
I	K	N	P	D	T	L	A	B	O	C	O
U	E	R	T	S	X	R	O	O	N	N	N
M	O	W	O	O	V	N	U	X	N	X	M
I	C	P	N	F	K	C	R	F	V	V	I
U	J	L	L	U	U	I	Z	R	F	E	C
M	T	D	H	M	G	Y	I	G	F	H	X

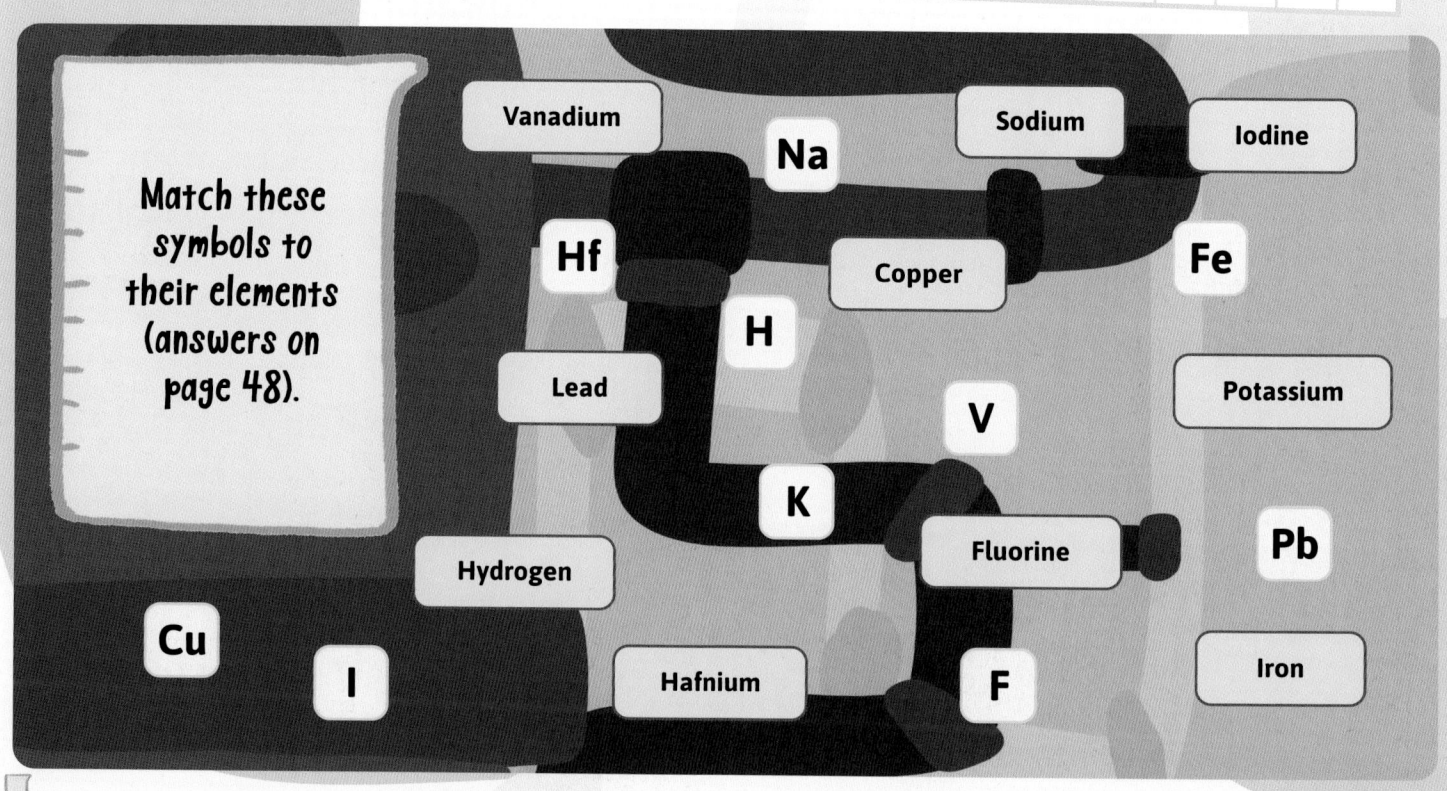

Match these symbols to their elements (answers on page 48).

Vanadium — Na — Sodium — Iodine

Hf — Copper — Fe

H

Lead — V — Potassium

K

Hydrogen — Fluorine — Pb

Cu — I — Hafnium — F — Iron

46

PERIODIC TABLE BATTLESHIP

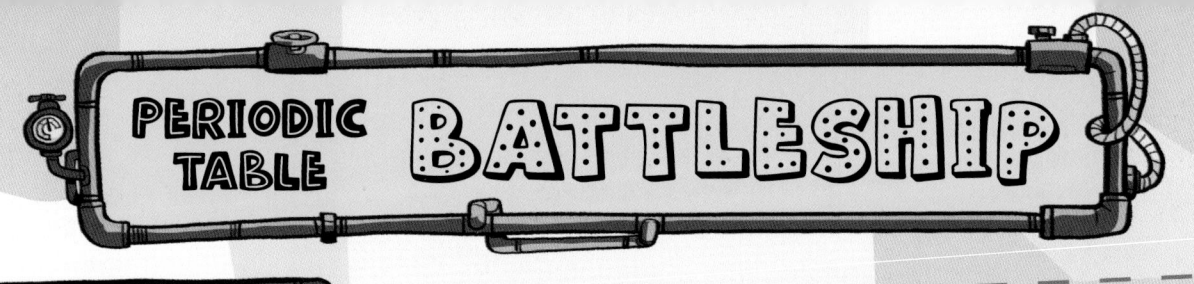

Grab a friend and play Periodic Table Battleship! You will need tracing paper or a photocopier, and two pencils.

1. Trace two copies of the table on pages 4–5 onto a piece of paper (or photocopy it twice if you are able to).
2. Each of you should draw four battleships, three elements long, one element wide, in different places on your periodic table – making sure your friend can't see you!
3. Take it in turns to guess an element that might be where one of your opponent's ships is stationed. If you choose an element on one of your opponent's ships, that's a hit. If you don't, that's a miss. Mark your table accordingly.
4. You need to work out all three elements per ship to sink it.
5. To win, sink all of your opponent's ships first, before yours have been destroyed.

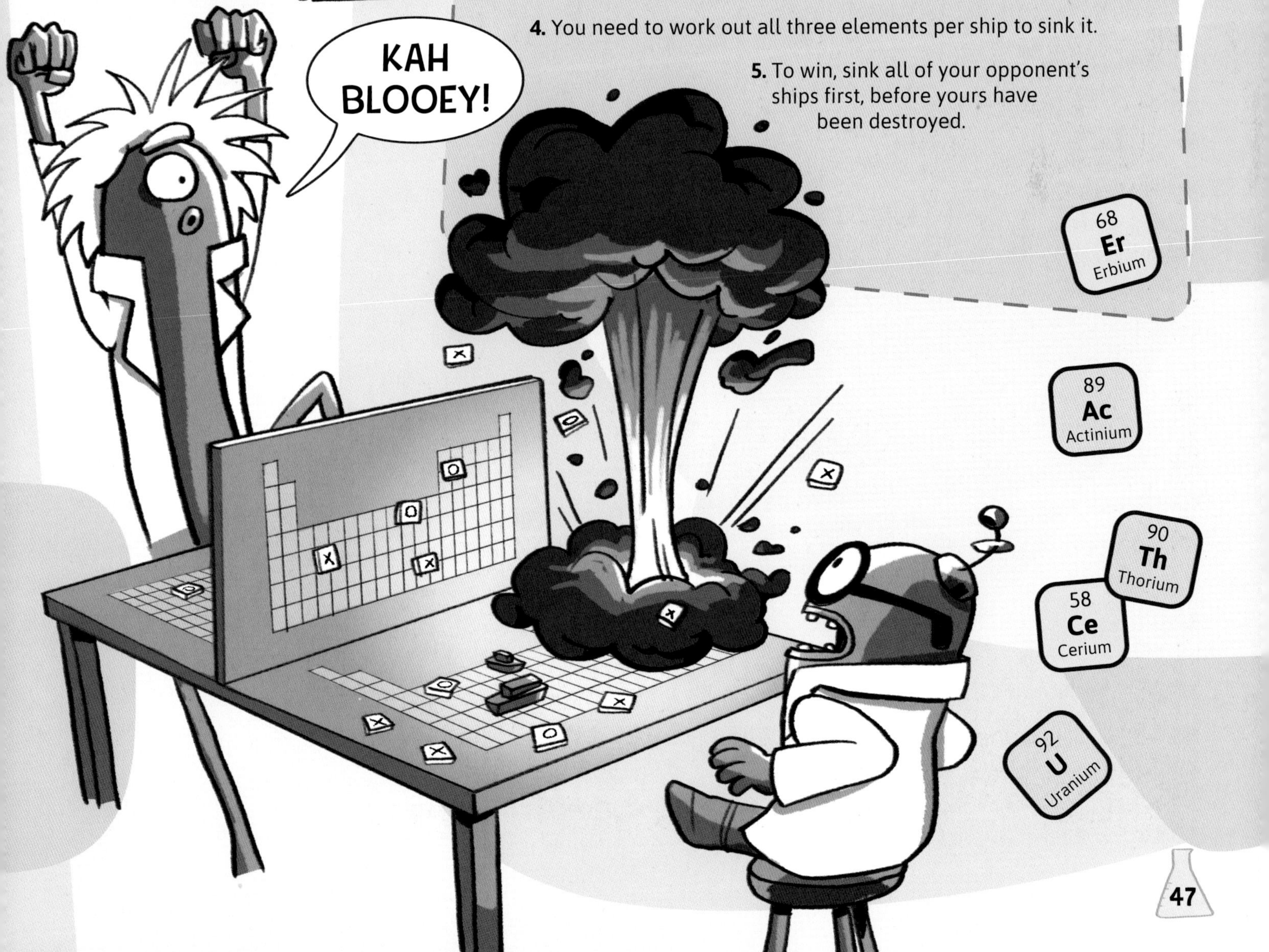
KAH BLOOEY!
68 Er Erbium
89 Ac Actinium
90 Th Thorium
58 Ce Cerium
92 U Uranium

INDEX

ANSWERS:

Matching symbols to elements

Copper Cu
Fluorine F
Iodine I
Hafnium Hf

Hydrogen H
Lead Pb
Potassium K
Sodium Na
Vanadium V